First Edition
Genuine Autographed Collectible

Do you want me to sign it in ink or in lipstick?

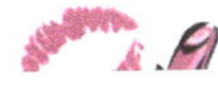

WIN
AT
THIN

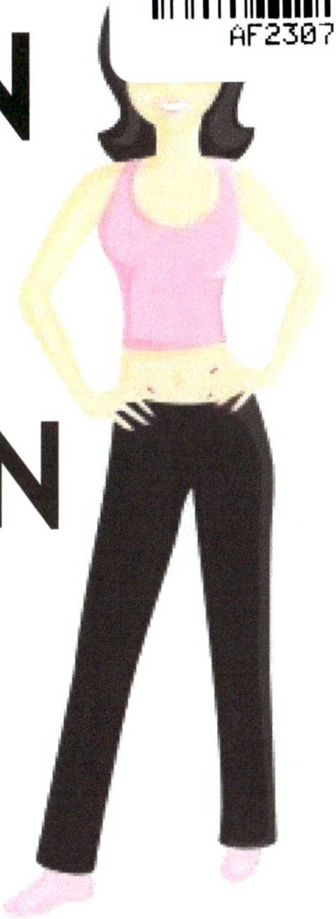

FAT ME
SKINNY ME

What Works!
What Doesn't Work!

Gift Card

Date:

To:

From:

Message:

What Do Books Do?

BOOKS ARE POWERFUL

Books Educate!
Books Enlighten!
Books Empower!
Books Emancipate!
Books Entertain!
Books Spring Eternal!
Books Drive Exploration!
Books Spark Evolution!
Books Ignite Revolution!

Sharon Esther Lampert

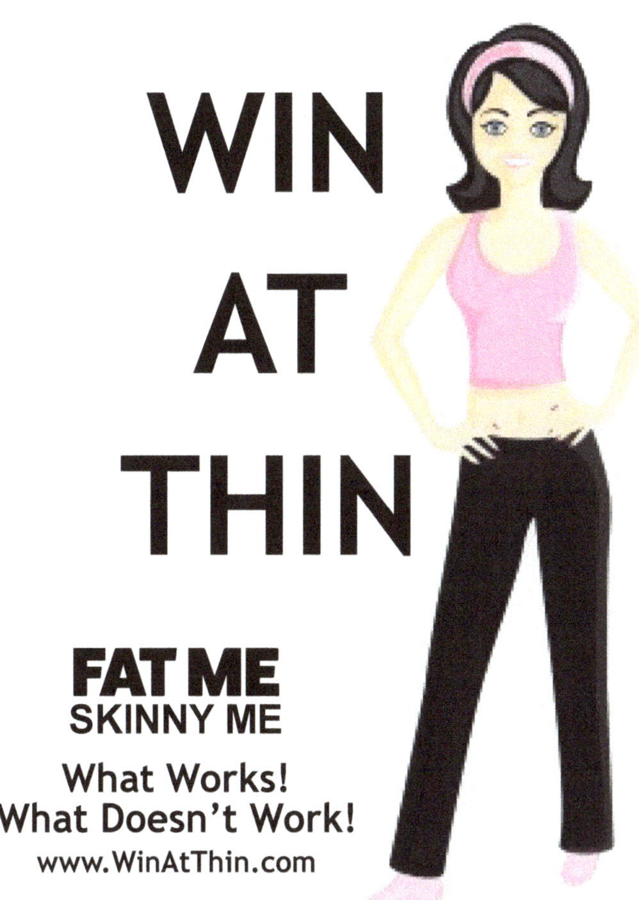
WIN
AT
THIN
FAT ME
SKINNY ME
What Works!
What Doesn't Work!
www.WinAtThin.com

Self-Help, Health, Nutrition, Diet, Exercise, Weight Loss, Sharon Esther Lampert

WIN AT THIN
FAT ME to SKINNY ME
What Works! What Doesn't Work!

KADIMAH PRESS
GIFTS OF GENIUS

Books may be purchased for education, business, or sales promotional use.
ISBN: Hardcover 978-1-885872-24-1
ISBN: Paperback 978-1-885872-25-8
ISBN: E-Book 978-1-885872-26-5
PCN: Library of Congress Control Number: 2019912602

FAN MAIL
www.SharonEstherLampert.com
www.WinAtThin.com
FANS@SharonEstherLampert.com

Global Online Websites for Orders and Distribution:
INGRAM, 1 Ingram Blvd. La Vergne, TN 37086-3629
Phone: 615-793-5000,
Fax orders: 615-287-6990

Book Design and Interior: Creative Genius Sharon Esther Lampert

Editor: Dave Segal

First Edition

Manufactured in the United States of America

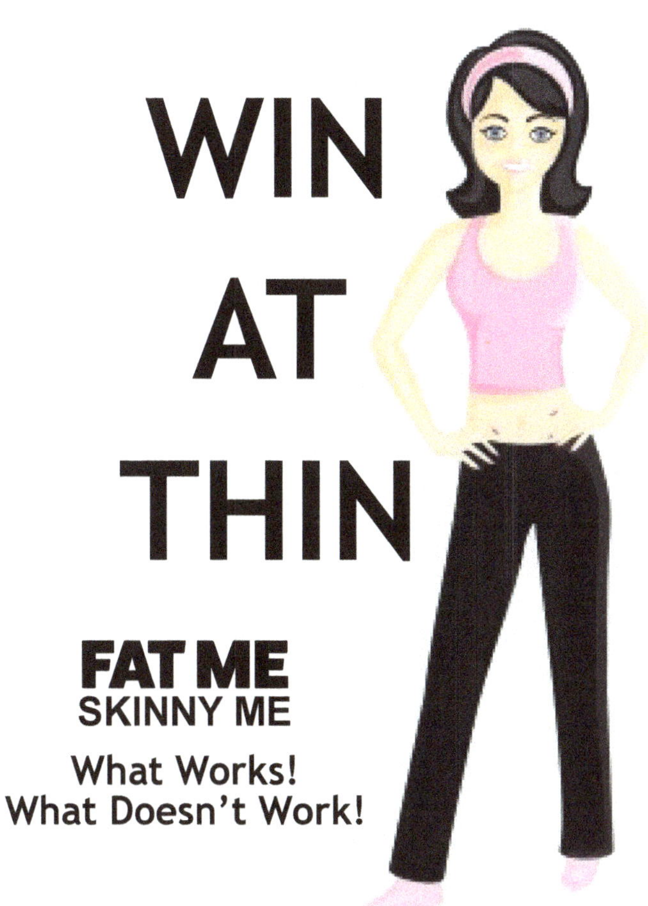

WIN
AT
THIN
FAT ME
SKINNY ME
What Works!
What Doesn't Work!

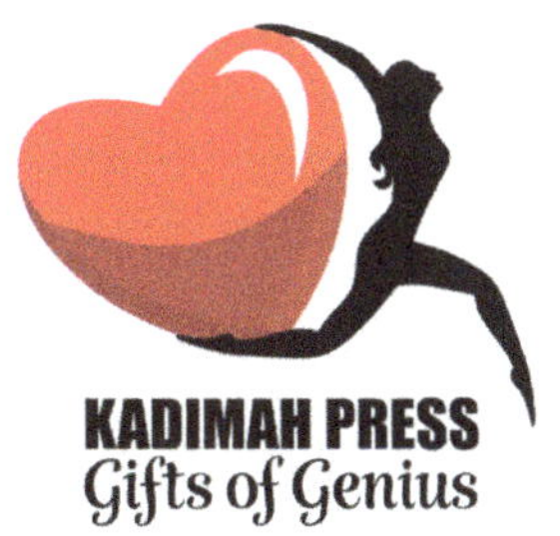

KADIMAH PRESS
Gifts of Genius

Awesome Art of Alliteration
Using One Letter of the Alphabet

What Do Books Do?
—Written in Letter E

8 Goalposts of Education
—Written in Letter E

Sharon's Biography
—Written in Letters F, B and P

No Fakes!
No Fat!
No Fluff!
No Filler!
No Flops!
No Fudge!
No F-Bomb!

CUPID
Language of Love
—Written in Letter C

TEMPORARY INSANITY
We Are All Building Our Lives on a Sand Trap
Make Life Make Sense
—Written in Letter S

THE SECRET SAUCE OF BOOK SALES
PUBLISH How to Make Money Selling Books
—Written in Letter P

DESTINY
Are You Living Life by Default or by Design?
—Written in Letter D

THERAPY
Every Day You Will Take a Test.
What Test Did You Take Today?
—Written in Letter T

POWER
Purgatory or Paradise?
—Written in Letter P

MOMMY
LOVE OF MY LIFETIME

Eve Paikoff Lampert
June 3, 1925 — May 5, 1985

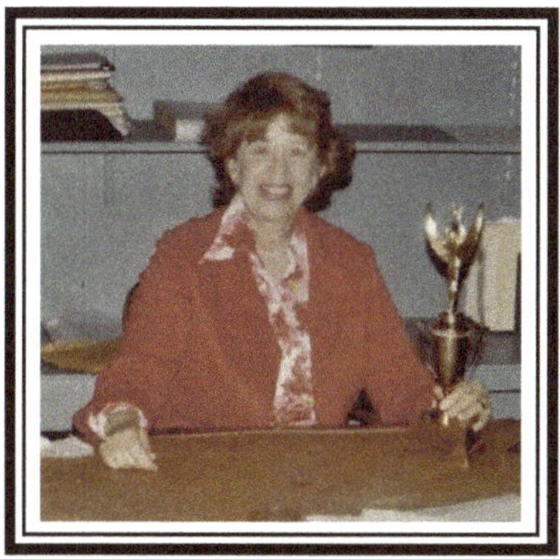

At Age 9

MOMMY
Knew Who I Was
From the INSIDE OUT!

"My daughter is a poet,
philosopher, and teacher.
Sharon is the Princess &
the Pea!"

Medical Disclaimer

WIN AT THIN diet book is purely intended to provide information hence should not under any circumstance substitute medical advice from a qualified physician or dietician.

WIN AT THIN diet book should not be used to diagnose or treat any medical condition. For diagnosis and treatment of any medical condition, please consult your physician. Before starting any diet, you should first talk to your doctor about it.

Statistics 2023

- According to the CDC, two-thirds (66%) of Americans are overweight or obese

- Average person starts a new diet 5-times a year

- 85% of people who buy diet products are women

- Most dieters regain lost weight in 1-5 years

- 75% of women harbor negative thoughts related to food and their body

- **SAD: S**tandard **A**merican **D**iet
  95% Processed Foods, 5% Fresh Fruits & Vegetables

Eat breakfast like a king.
Eat lunch like a prince.
Eat dinner like a pauper.

—Adelle Davis

Table of Contents

Favorite Quotes

"When diet is wrong, medicine is of no use.
When diet is correct, medicine is of no need."
  —Ayurvedic proverb

"Eat food, not too much, mostly plants."
  —Michael Pollan

"It's not what you're eating; it's what's eating you!"
  —Unknown

"All disease begins in the gut."
  –Ancient Greek physician Hippocrates, 2500 years ago

"One fateful morning, I looked at myself in the mirror and realized that I shouldn't be operating on patients and then teaching them to eat to avoid me in the future; I should teach them to eat so that I wouldn't have to operate on them in the first place!"
  —Dr. Steven Gundry

Introduction

When I joined a Florida gym, there was a group of five 300-pound obese young women in their early 20s who regularly joined my spin class.

After some chit-chat in the women's locker room, there was one mistake that kept repeating itself — the ghastly mistake of guzzling down sugary soda all day — for years!

After hours of hard work in the gym — riding spin bikes for hours — and after losing 100 pounds, they covered their arms with plastic-garbage bags, as their stretched-out skin was sagging — and in need of cosmetic surgery.

They would purchase a new set of used clothes at the thrift shop after every 25 pounds of weight loss.

At 200 pounds they still had another 50 pounds to go before cosmetic surgery. They downsized from size 22 to 8!

- They learned to drink water with a squeeze of lemon or lime with a hint of ginger and drizzle of honey!
- They learned how eat fiber to control their blood sugar!
- They learned the difference between macronutrients and micronutrients!
- They learned to eat nutrient-dense, low-caloric whole food without ingredient labels!
- They learned how to eat small portions of organic good proteins, good carbohydrates, and good fats!
- The most important lesson of all — they learned positive self-talk, how to believe in themselves, and how to love themselves through the 5-year transformation from **FAT ME** to SKINNY ME BRAVA!

These obese women inspired me to write this book. This book is one of a kind as it ellucidates the significant transformations in mind, body, and spirit in an original way.

If this book made a difference in your life, please contact me with your success story: FANS@WinAtThin.com

Sharon Esther Lampert
Author, Athlete, and Activist

FAT ME: What Doesn't Work!

Breakfast: 1500+ Calories

I run out the door with no fuel in my tank, and leave myself vulnerable to the temptations of fast food, processed food, fried food, bakery goods, and junk food. The first meal of the day is my drive-through chocolate-cream filled donut.

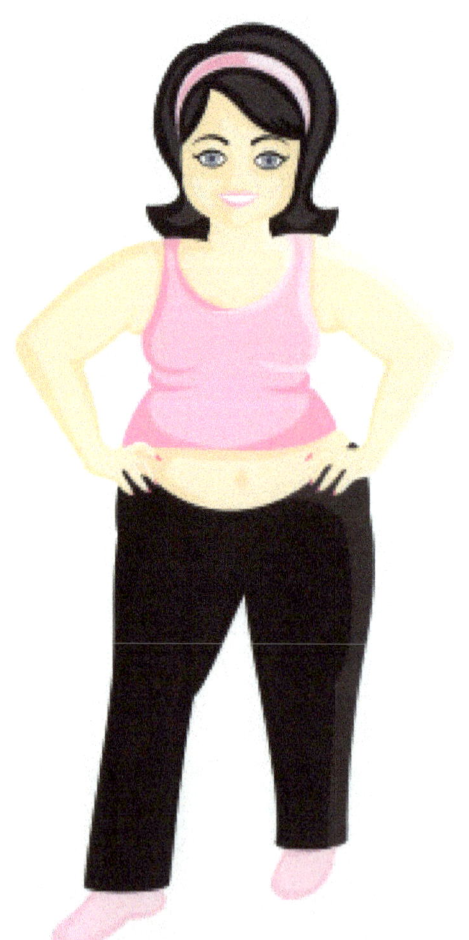

In an hour, I will be famished... and looking for my next fix... I am a sugar addict!

My Breakfast Options:
Wherever the temptation leads me... 1500 calories at every meal... I filler-up on empty calories:

- Fast Food
- Junk Food
- Processed Food
- Fried Food
- Bakery Pastries
- Restaurant Meal:
  Each portion feeds two or even three people!

Total Calories: 1500+ Per Meal

WIN AT THIN

Skinny Me: What Works!

Breakfast: 250-500 Calories

I never leave home on an empty stomach.
I eat a fiber-rich meal that regulates my blood
sugar, and provides sustained energy.
I am satiated — never hungry!
I am fortified with vitamins and minerals.

I am bulletproof — free of food addition.

There are no false-advertising fast-food billboards
that can lure me into
their trap on my
way to work.

4 Rules:
Hints!
Squirts!
Sprinkles!
& Drizzles!

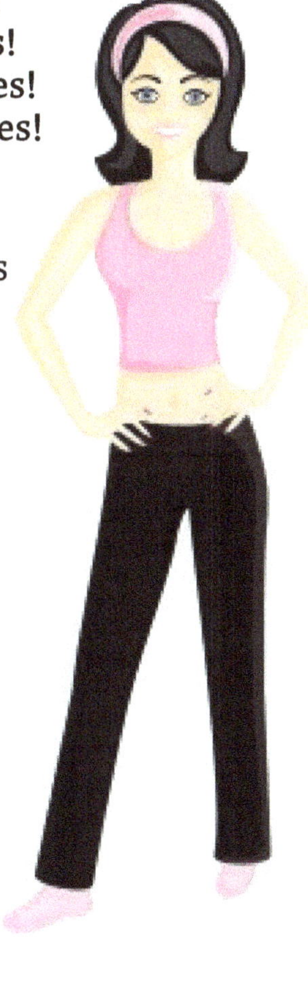

My Breakfast Options:

FIBER: Nutrient-Dense Whole Foods

- Good Protein: 2 Hard-Boiled Eggs
- Good Fat: Avocado
- Good Carbohydrate: Oatmeal
  - Slice 1/4 Banana & Blueberries
  - Sprinkle Wheat Germ
  - Sprinkle Flax Seeds
  - Sprinkle Hemp Seeds
  - Sprinkle Cinnamon & Cardamom Spice
  - Drizzle of Maple Syrup

- My Favorite Green Drink:
  Celery, Green Apple, Cinnamon,
  Ginger & Protein Powder

Total Calories: 250-500 Per Meal

FAT ME: What Doesn't Work!

Lunch: I'm Always Starving! Why Is That?

At 12 p.m., I run out of the office famished because my breakfast did not contain FIBER the filler-upper.
The second meal of the day is another high-caloric meal of 1,500 calories from a local eatery that consists of processed meat, processed cheese, and processed white bread stripped of all nutrients. At the very least, I am economically supporting the local businesses in my community.

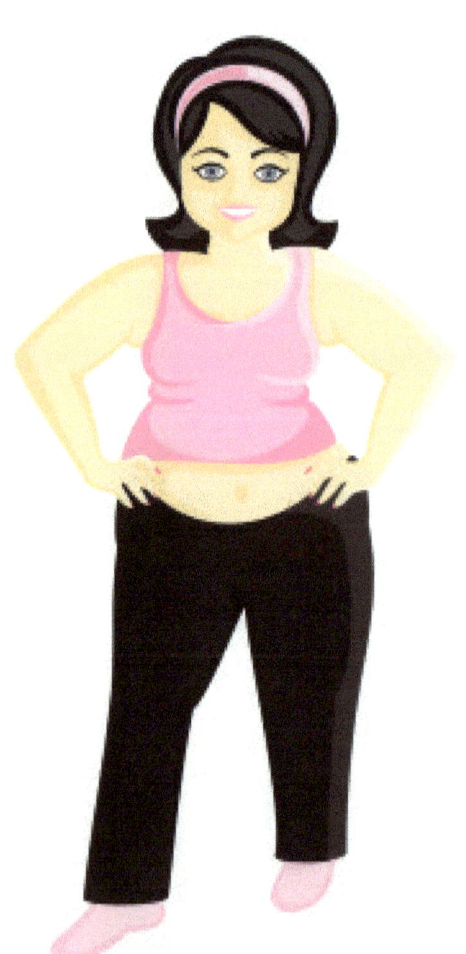

Instead of using **FIBER** to **ENERGIZE**—

I am eating foods that do not give me the **FUEL** I need to accomplish my daily activities.

- I am sluggish!
- I am always tired!
- I keep junk food in my purse …
- I drink 2-3 cups of coffee a day!
- I don't sleep well— too much caffiene!
- I am tired! Repeat!

Skinny Me: What Works!

Lunch: I'll Skip it for an Early Dinner!

My FIBER-filled breakfast is giving me the FUEL
I need to skip lunch — and have an early dinner at
5 p.m. Dinner: Good Protein & Veggies.

I always have a bottle of water in my bag
to keep me hydrated during the day. I add lemon,
ginger, and a hint of honey, nutritious and delicious!

Emotional Eating Gameplan:

It was a stressful day — and
I deal with my stress by
grabbing a handful (1/4 cup)
of savory-crunchy nuts:

- Pecans
- Almonds
- Pistashios

APPLES never get boring,
as they come in more than
30 varieties — from sweet to
tart. One apple is usually enough!

CLEMENTINES are easy to
peel, and are nutrient rich
filled with FIBER and
loaded with vitamins.

DATES are a great option too!

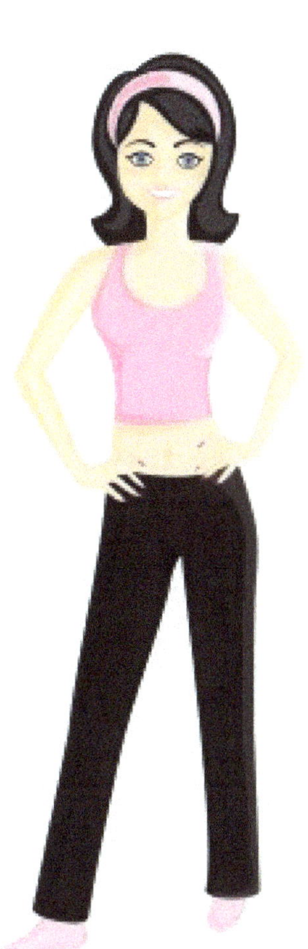

FAT ME: What Doesn't Work!

Food Coma: I'm Full! I'm Bloated! I'm Fat!

I eat dinner late — and go to bed on a full stomach.
I eat a 3-course meal, and look forward to dessert.
I continue to munch on processed snacks until bedtime.
I am an emotional eater and I have a sweet tooth!
I catch up on the news of the day, and it is always rife with
horror stories that create stress, anxiety, and depression.
I can't watch any of it without my bag of chips and dip.

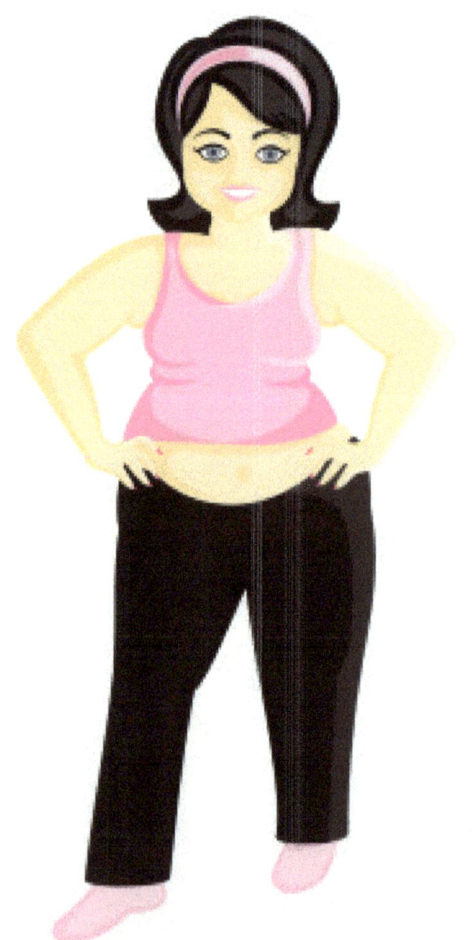

I purchase boxes of
cookies on sale. It was
a great deal that I
could not pass up!
I also have milk
chocolate bars on
standby for a sweet
tooth emergency!
There are also the
leftover cakes from
family get-togethers.
The expiration date
is coming due — another
reason to eat eat every
last cookie and crumb!

Skinny Me: What Works!

Dinner: I Eat to Energize! Berrylicious!

I eat an early dinner, 4-6 p.m. I don't eat dessert, except on rare occassions, in celebration of an annual birthday or holiday. People, the world over are obsessed with sweets. I do love sweets, but prefer to enjoy fresh fruits packed with vitamins that will boost my energy reserves, and build my immune system:

- **Blueberries**
- **Raspberries**
- **Strawberries**
- **Cherries**

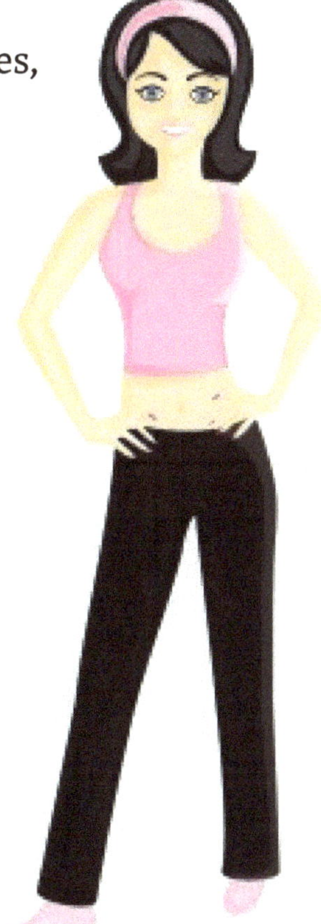

I gave up processed cakes and cookies, when it dawned on me that I was eating three cups of sugar and two sticks of butter in every bite.

Ask yourself this question:

Do you want to eat three cups of sugar and two sticks of butter?

Of course not! **ZERO** nutrition! Sugar is an addictive drug!

I watch the daily news once a week because it is too toxic!

I don't know why they don't report on the good news of the day!

What **BLEEDS** leads... **STRESS**!

FAT ME: What Doesn't Work!

Science 101: How Do I Lose Weight?

If I want to lose weight, I must create some form of calorie deficit and eat fewer calories than I burn. I need to eat less calories, but still get the proper nutrition to be healthy. A registered dietian is a good idea if you have underlying health issues and vitamin deficiencies.

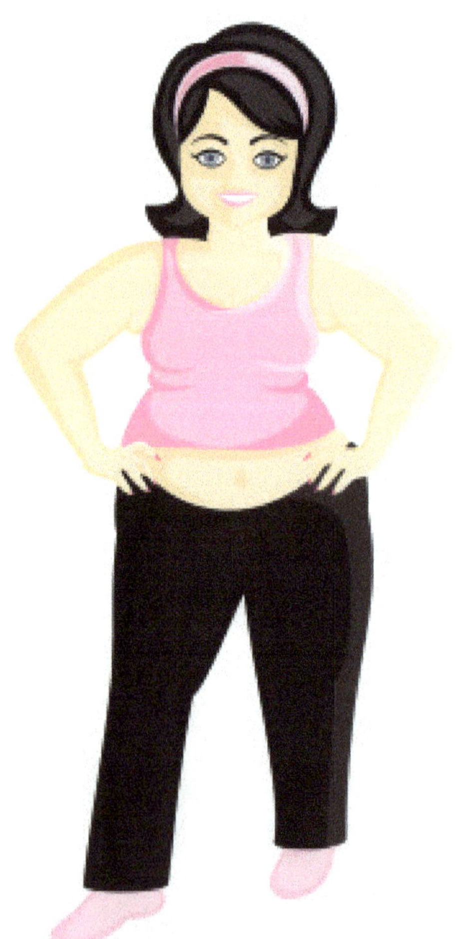

There is No One Formula for Everybody. There is Just One Formula for You!

Obese people begin by talking long walks. Going to a gym can be emotionally difficult.

- Get a trainer!
- Get a dietian!
- Ask a doctor to approve your gym routine!

There are gyms that have weight rooms:

FOR WOMEN ONLY!

Skinny Me: What Works!

Self-Care 101: Self-Care is Not Selfish!

To maintain my zest for life and living, I am cognizant of the complex equation of variables that contribute to my wellbeing:

My Self-Love Formula:

- Positive Self-Talk

- Ground Energy Edibles — From Nature Not a Factory No Ingredient Labels — Labels are Often Misleading!

- Supplements to Enhance My Diet

- Exercise: Exertion & Recovery

- Find the Helpers! Ignore Naysayers! Ignore Haters! Ignore Fearmongers!

- Listen to MUSIC instead of NEWS!

- Sleep: Regular Bedtime

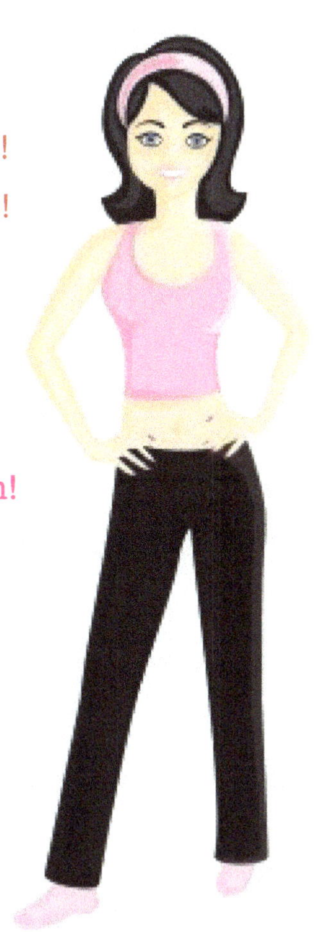

Good People, Nothing is a Problem! Bad People, Everything is a Problem!

—Philosopher Queen Sharon Esther Lampert

Lesson: Supplements 101

Don't try to fix a poor diet by taking 50+ different supplements. Supplements are not food! You cannot survive in the jungle on supplements! Supplements are enhancements to a good diet of whole foods!

FAT ME: What Doesn't Work!

My Childhood Menu: A National Crisis!

At home, we ate whatever our parents fed us.
In school, we ate whatever our teachers fed us.
In childhood, we didn't have a choice:

I ate everything that was put on my plate!

If you are Italian, every meal had pasta and cheese. If you are Russian, you ate a lot of potatoes. If you are Latin, you ate a lot of white rice.

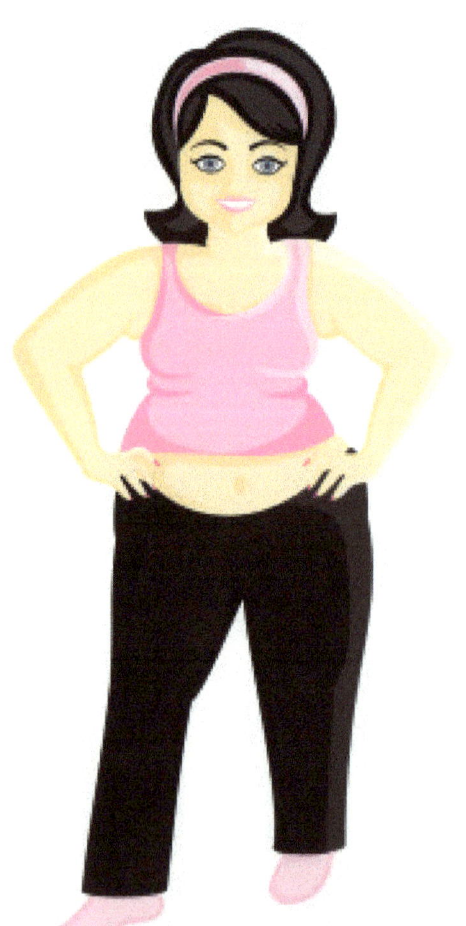

If you are African American, everything you ate was fried — including a pickle.

In school, they didn't even teach us about nutrition, They still don't!

Obesity is a National Crisis!

By age 5, most of my generation were addicted to sugar: CANDY!

Skinny Me: What Works!

How to Visit My Family During Meals

As an adult, I began paying attention to what my family was putting on my dinner plate during meals and special holidays.

1st Problem: Oversized portions!
2nd Problem: Too many fried foods!
3rd Problem: Meals are overcooked and reduce the potency of vitamins & minerals!
4th Problem: Food preparation: Each meal is 2,500+ calories!

The easiest solution is to eat at home, and visit my family and say, "I ate already, but I would love to sit at the table and chat."

I don't like being tempted and tormented by high-caloric foods with empty calories, and then pack on 5 pounds of weight! I can only change myself!

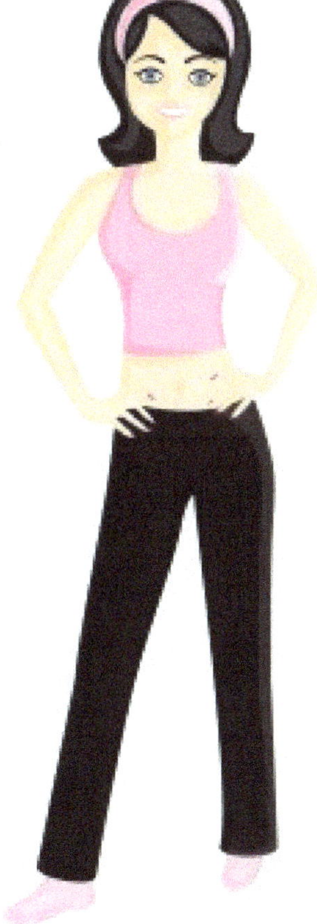

FAT ME: What Doesn't Work!

Unconscious Eating Habits

Eating healthy sounds like a good idea. I have to learn to say, "Yes!" and, "No!" "Yes!" is easy. "No!" is the hard part. I like most foods. I am not a finicky eater. I will eat almost anything you put on my plate! Thanks to globalization, **processed foods** from every country in the world are within my reach in the frozen-food section of my supermarket:

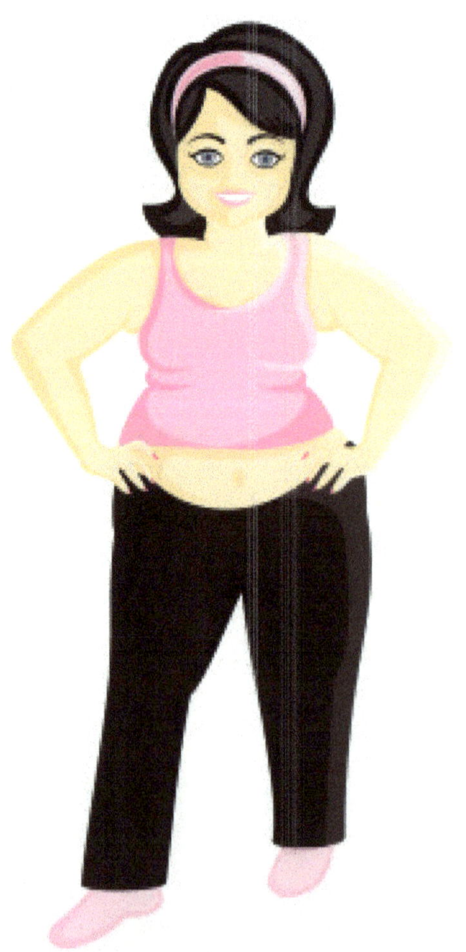

- Chinese Yummy!
- Thai Yummy!
- Japanese Yummy!
- Mexican Burito Yummy!
- Greek Yummy!
- Jewish & Israeli Yummy!
- Korean Yummy!
- American Hotdog & Hamburger Yummy!
- Italian Yummy!
- Polish Yummy!
- Swedish Yummy!

Processed food is always on sale! I have a big freezer! I plan on eating it all!

Skinny Me: What Works!

Conscious Eating Habits

I never leave home on an empty stomach!
I make sure I am full so that I will be able to resist all the temptations! The grocery store places sugary-processed foods in the front of the store. I have to walk by them — there is no other choice! The pretty cakes are always on sale too! **2 for \$5 3 for \$10   5 for \$15**

On my grocery shopping excursions, I prepare a well-defined list of healthy foods and stick to my list. I avoid impulse buys that make me spend more money and overrun my budget. I don't want to add more debt to my credit card, and more fat to my tummy — a LOSE-LOSE game plan!

My Grocery List:

- Bottled Water
- Frozen & Fresh Vegetables
- Frozen & Fresh Fruits
- Lean Proteins
- Fresh Garlic & Ginger
- Crumbled Cheeses (sprinkle)

FAT ME: What Doesn't Work!

Digestion 101: Where Does the Food Go?

Science & biology were not my favorite subjects in school. I regret not paying more attention to how my body works. I live in my body 24-HOURS a DAY, 7-DAYS a WEEK for life!

What happens to the food I place in my mouth?

Lesson 1. **My Body**

Step 1. Mouth: Saliva & Chewing
Step 2. Esophagus: Swallowing
Step 3. Stomach: Digestive Acid
Step 4. Small Intestine: Peristalsis
Step 5. Large Intestine (waste)
      Colon, Rectum & Anus

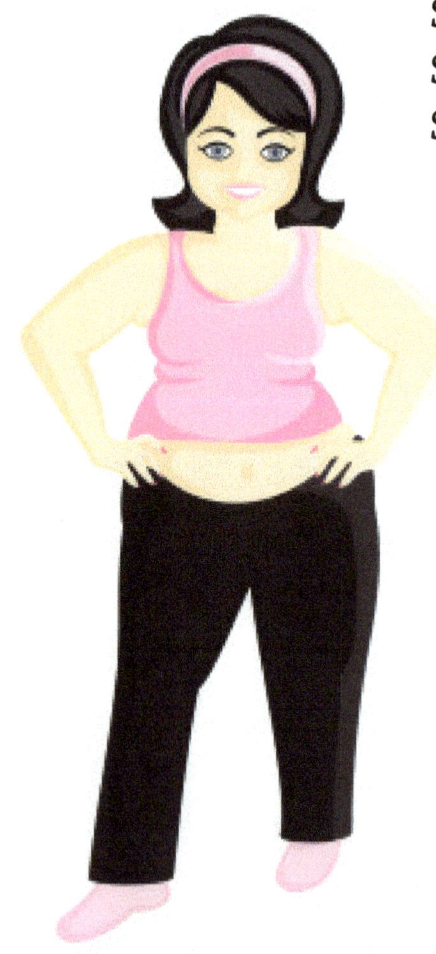

Lesson 2. **Digestion**

Food is broken down into carbohydrates, proteins, fats and vitamins. Nutrients are absorbed into my blood stream and carried to cells in my body.

Lesson 3. **Energy**

My body uses nutrients for energy, growth, and cell repair.

Skinny Me: What Works!

Never Leave Home on an Empty Stomach

Some mornings are too harried to stop and make a nutritious & delicious breakfast. Advance preparation: make healthy meals for the next day, week — or month.

Inevitably, I may have to stop and purchase something to eat, and put myself at risk for indulging in fast food or junk food, e.g., sugary, salty or fried foods.

Plan A. 15 Minute Meal
Eggs & Veggies (Pasture-Raised Eggs)

Plan B. 10 Minute Meal
A bowl of oatmeal with fiber-fuel: crispy apples & blueberries. E-Z: Make the oatmeal the night before — then microwave it for 30 seconds in the morning.

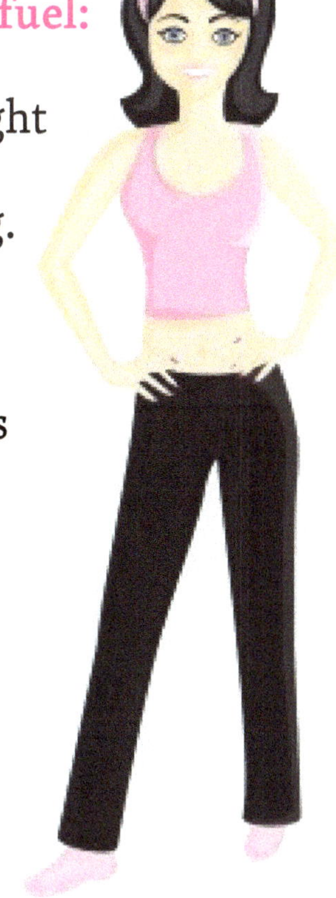

Plan C. 5 Minute Meal
GrabNGo!
- Microwave 2 Eggs & Veggies
- Clementine & Apple
- 2 Bottles of Water

Plan D. 1 Minute Meal
GrabNGo!
- 2 Hard-Boiled Eggs
- Clementine & Apple
- 2 Bottles of Water

FAT ME: What Doesn't Work!

Food is a Major Labor Intensive Effort

It seems to be the case, that every living being knows who and what to eat — except us human beings.

Why are most of us overweight or obese?

I was raised in an urban metropolis — not on a farm.

I do not know how to grow anything!

I can't imagine going out on a boat and fishing for my dinner at the crack of dawn.

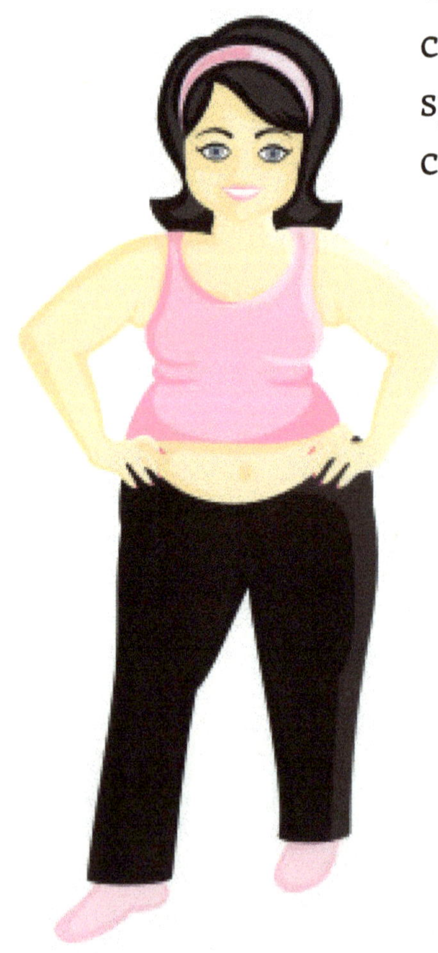

I can't imagine learning how capture a wild animal — or spending hours, cleaning, cutting cooking, and freezing raw meat. I also can't imagine having to milk a cow. If I had to prepare my food by first having to grow my food — I would only eat fresh fruits and vegetables. I am a wuss! **I have to rethink every morsal I put into my mouth!** I have to rethink how much food do I really need to eat each day!

Skinny Me: What Works!

Inverse Proportions: 3/4 Vegetables

There are three macronutrients:

Protein, Carbohydrates, and Fats.

In childhood, I was served a large piece of chicken, and a small side dish of vegetables:

3/4 Protein & 1/4 Vegetable

In restaurants, they serve every meal with the exact same proportions, and serve fewer vegetables!

As an adult, I decided that these proportions were all wrong!

A plant-based diet is the healthiest choice.

First, I choose my vegetable:
- Broccoli
- Green Beans
- Spinach or Kale
- Mixed Vegetables

Second, I add a lean protein:
- Chicken, Fish, Eggs, Turkey

My New Proportions!
- 3/4 of My Plate Is Vegetables
- 1/4 of My Plate Is Protein

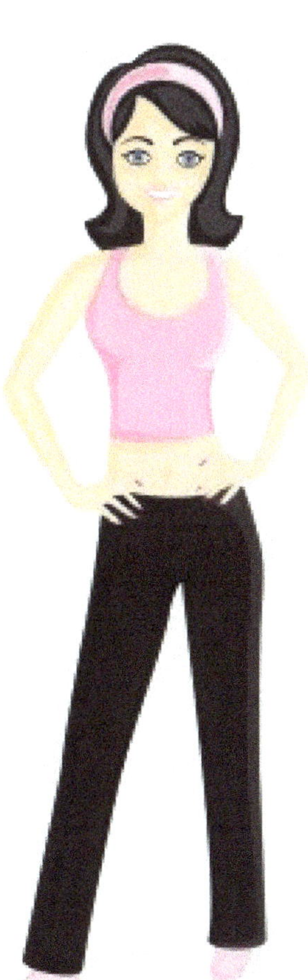

FAT ME: What Doesn't Work!

Nutrition 101: What Does My Body Need?

I did not learn an iota about nutrition at home from my parents — or at school from my teachers.

My friends share their recipes, but 99.9% of the dishes are delicious — but not nutritious! IT'S ALL UP TO ME!

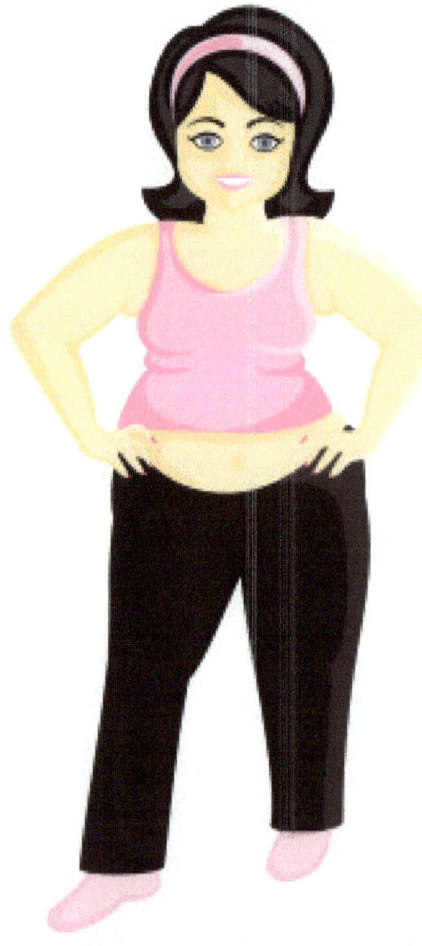

Lesson 1.

There are 3 macronutrients and 2 micronutrients.

Lesson 2.

- 3 Macronutrients: Protein Carbohydrates, and Fats.
- Protein: 9 Essential Amino Acids 11 Non-Essential Amino Acids
- Carbohydrates: Sugar, Starch & Fiber
- Fats: Saturated or Unsaturated

Lesson 3.

2 Micronutrients: Vitamins & Minerals.

Lesson 4.

1. Vitamins: A, C, D, K, and

B Complex: B6, B12, and Folate

Lesson 5.

2. Minerals: Calcium, Sodium, and Potassium. Trace Minerals: Copper, Iodine, and Zinc

Skinny Me: What Works!

Read Food Labels: Good & Bad Choices

Read the entire front and back label of every product that you purchase:

1. If you do not understand the ingredients on the back label — **DO NOT BUY THE PRODUCT!**
2. If "Sugar..." is the first ingredient on the back label — **DO NOT BUY THE PRODUCT!**

Too often, the front label states that the product is the healthiest product in the marketplace, however, the back label states in very small print that requires a magnifying glass that the product contains artificial ingredients like chemical preservatives, fillers, and additives.

A healthy & delicious plate of vegetables covered in a tasty salad dressing containing sugar & salt, and chemical preservatives is a **BIG NO! NO!**

FAT ME: What Doesn't Work!

You Can't Out Exercise a Bad Diet!

Last time I visited the gym, my trainer was in the middle of a conversation with another member — and I sat down nearby to wait it out. I could overhear the exchange. The topic discussed was how to caluculate how may hours of exercise for every wrong food choice.

Q. How many hours on the bike if I eat a glazed donut?

Q. How many hours on the bike if I eat a slice of pizza?

Q. How many hours on the bike if I eat birthday cake?

Q. How many hours on the bike if I pig out on a whole bag of chips?

The answers to the questions was beyond belief! It takes time to burn off calories! Your body uses the calories for energy or stores the calories as fat!

80% Diet — 20% Exercise!

Skinny Me: What Works!

Eat Right Every Single Day, All Day Long

As I watch the excess pounds come off, I feel great! I can now look at myself in the mirror, and enjoy my reflection! I take a **SELFIE!**

This is also a spiritual journey. This is my favorite mantra to help me stay on track:

Passion with a Purpose! Be Patient!

Be Positive! Build Perseverance! = Progress!

I rewrite the soundtrack inside my head to build my new relationship to food:

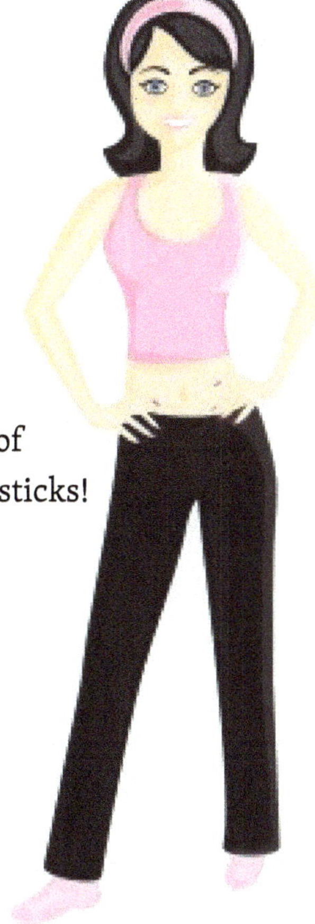

- Food is Fuel! ENERGIZE!
- Food is Medicine or Poison!
- **Eat the Foods You LOVE That LOVE You Back!**
- Food is Energy Used or Stored as Fat!
- Emotional Eating: I binge on my love of blueberries, apple slices, and celery sticks!
- Never Leave Home on an Empty Stomach! FILLER-UP FIBER!
- Food Journal: Keep Track of Food Choices & Energy Level
- Take a fabulous SELFIE!

All day long, I have to make the right decisions as to what to eat to stay lean, fit, and energized!

FAT ME: What Doesn't Work!

Living to Eat or Eating to Live?

The only time I see my family and friends are when we get together to share a meal.

When I date, it is always a get together at a new restaurant for a fabulous meal.

Our eating routines are all about dining and conversations about this, that, and the other.

Meals Are Really About Socializing!

If I want to network, it is best to invite friends out for lunch. They will make time — because they have to eat, and enjoy the free food at their favorite restaurant.

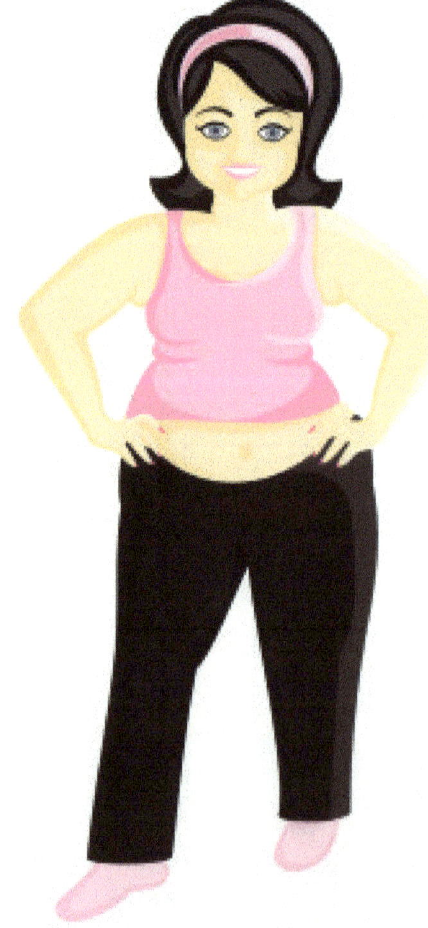

Restaurant meals are usually too big to finish.

Lesson 1. Eat at Home
Eat Before You Eat Out!

Lesson 2. Cut in Half
As soon as the entree is served, cut it in half and take it home. I love leftovers! Yummy!

Lesson 3. Share Entree
Either pass an entree around table buffet style or share an entree — no food to take home!

Skinny Me: What Works!

Eat Foods You Love That Love You Back

As I shop, I can't help noticing that I will bypass 3/4 of the food sold in the supermarket.

I pick up a box of chocolate donuts and give the box a hug. I walk around with the box of donuts — and later place it back on the shelf. I talk to the donuts…

This is a one-way love affair! I can't take you home! I let go!

Sugar is an addictive drug! I will eat one donut — and in a matter of days, empty out the box. **I will be fat — not full!**

Lesson 1.
Out of Sight, Out of Mind!

Lesson 2.
Crush Your Cravings!

Lesson 3.
HARD CHOICES!
Elimination or Moderation?

Lesson 4.
No Gobbling! No Guzzling!

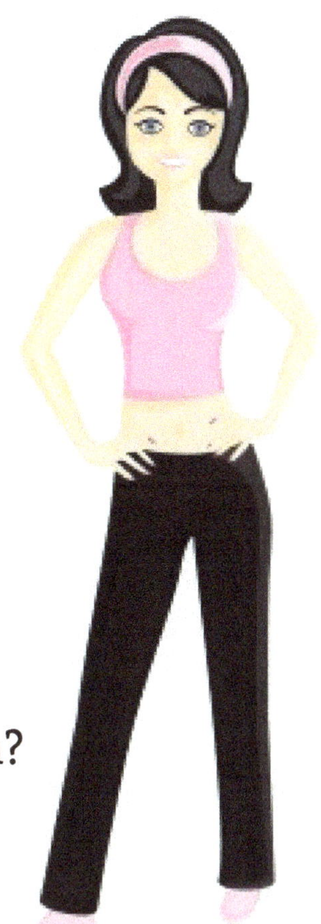

FAT ME: What Doesn't Work!

You Heard Me! I Check My POOP Every Day!

I am changing almost everything ... not easy!

Every morning, I start my day with this routine:

- Rise and pee! **Perfect POOP means I'm hydrated!**
- I drink water with lemon and ginger (drizzle of honey).
- I take my supplements: B12, Biotin, Vitamin C, Calcium Citrate, Magnesium, & Zinc, and a Women's Probiotic.
- I prepare a fiber-fueled breakfast of oatmeal with sliced bananas and a cup of blueberries.

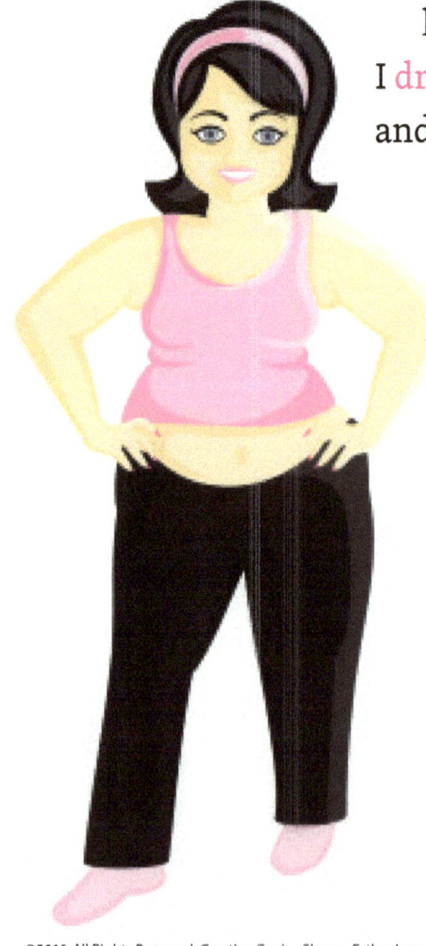

I add a sprinkle of flax seeds, hemp seeds, and wheat germ. I drizzle a hint of maple syrup and a squirt of milk. **YUMMY!** I drink a cup of coffee! I treat myself like a car. I have to fill up the gas tank if I want to drive. I don't want to start my day on an empty tank of **hunger pains & growls,** and then start looking for food. I do not want to be interrupted at work! Within a hour, I relieve myself and check my poop! **Perfect POOP is the start of a great day!**

Skinny Me: What Works!

Grocery Shopping to Feed My Gut Biome

I shop for groceries 2X times a month: frozen vegetables!
I buy seasonal frozen fruits & vegetables that are on sale!
I prefer to stock up on the big bags of organic vegetables
and organic fruits — and store them in my freezer.

- Mix of Spinach & Kale
- Broccoli Florets
- Mixed Medley of Vegetables
- Greenbeans
- Brussel Sprouts
- Dark Cherries
- Mixed Medley of Berries

I also slice & dice fresh fruits
and store them in my freezer:
- Bananas • Pineapples • Lemons
- Watermelon • Blueberries

I purchase a bag of garlic and a
jar of sun-dried tomatoes. I love
eating vegetables sauteed in garlic.

I stock up on lean proteins:
- Grass-Fed Beef & Wild-Caught Fish
- Eggs • Chicken • Fish • Meat
- Protein Power for Smoothies
- Crumbled Cheeses for Veggies

My Daily Snacks:
- Celery Sticks
- Carrots & Humus
- Apples & Peanut Butter
- Cucumbers & Cherry Tomatoes

**My Monthly Food Bill:
$250-$300 a Month**
- No Junk Food!
- No Processed Food!
- No Fast Food!
- No Sweets!

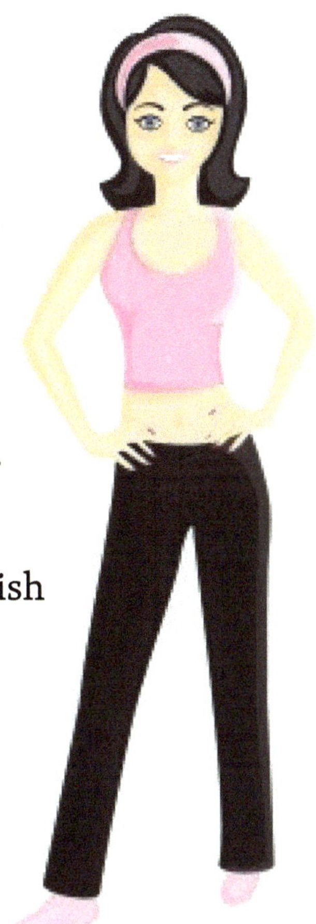

FAT ME: What Doesn't Work!

Juicing or Smoothies? BIG DIFFERENCE!

One of the most decadent drinks is a glass of fresh-squeezed orange juice at $5 a glass. I used to buy the packaged gallons of fresh orange juice until a "BREAKING NEWS STORY!" broke that it really wasn't, "FRESH FROM THE GROVE!" HEARTBREAKING! (sits in a storage facility for 6 months).

Drinking fresh juices without the PULP is losing out on the Fiber-Fuel!

In childhood, my obese friends went on liquid diets to lose weight. This was a good idea! Today, it is not uncommon to hear that a friend had gastric surgery to shed excess weight. This is usually the last option if you can't learn how to eat properly & exercise! They abhore exercise!

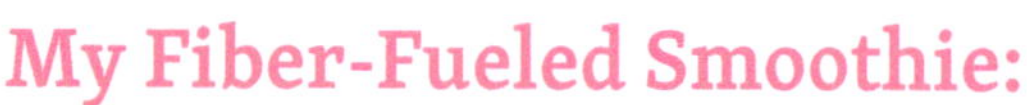

My Fiber-Fueled Smoothie:
- Water or Almond Milk
- Half a Banana (creamy texture)
- Half an Avocado (good fat)
- Greens; Mix of Kale & Spinach
- Fruit: Frozen Dark Cherries
- Sprinkle of Cinnamon & Flax Seeds

Skinny Me: What Works!

10-Minute Healthy Fast-Food Recipes

I do not want to spend more than 20 minutes in the kitchen preparing meals and washing dishes.
I designed healthy fast-food meals that are nutritious and delicious — and most importantly fuss free!

It takes me 10 minutes to prepare a healthy meal — and 5 minutes to eat a healthy meal.

Cooking is a Creative Art!

In my case, I would rather spend my time reading a good book. Every day, I use my freezer, microwave, and blender to prepare my daily meals.

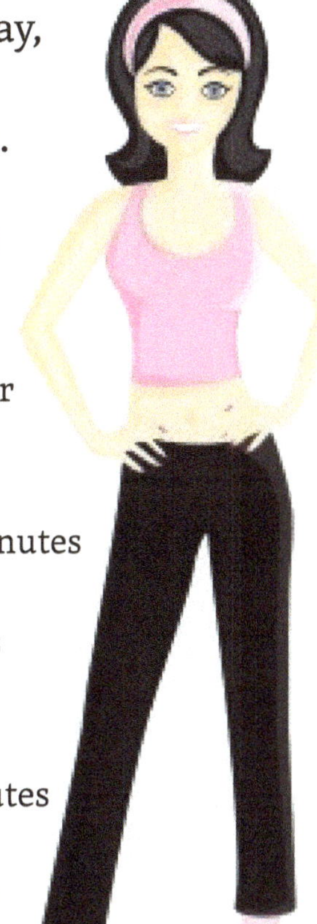

Breakfast Healthy Fast Food:

- 2 Eggs: 2 Minutes in a Microwave
- Oatmeal: 2 Minutes in a Microwave
- Green Smoothie: 1 Minute in a Blender

Lunch Healthy Fast Food:

- Frozen Vegetables, Microwave 3-4 Minutes
- Crumbled Goat Cheese: 5 Seconds
- 1 Can of Smoked Sardines: 10 Seconds

Dinner Healthy Fast Food:

- Frozen Vegetables, Microwave 3 Minutes
- Saute Garlic: 1-2 Minutes
- Sun-Dried Tomatoes (jar): 10 Seconds
- Grill Fish or Steak: 5 Minutes
- Sour Pickle (jar): 10 Seconds

FAT ME: What Doesn't Work!

My Childhood Exercise Routine

As a kid, my exercise routine was exactly the same as all of my friends in the neighborhood. No one had a gym in their home! In school, my exercise was planned by my teachers. On weekends, I joined a sport's team. We were guzzling gallons of sugary sodas! We were junk-food obsessed kids!

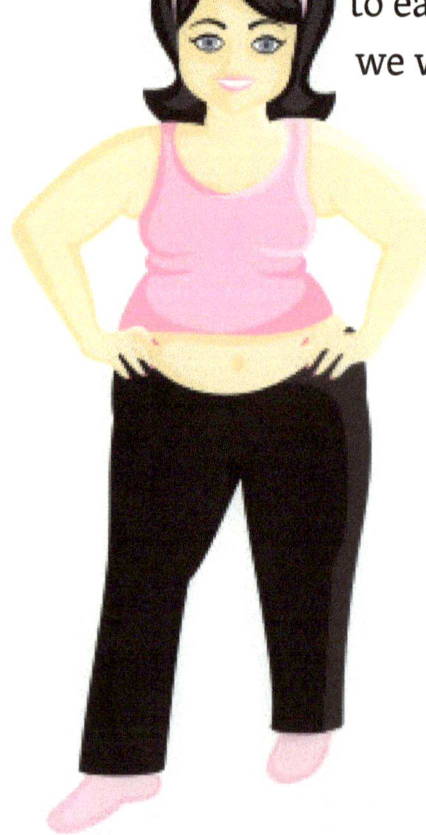

We never talked about how much food we were supposed to eat, and how much exercise we were supposed to do to burn off our fat calories. I had to learn how to lose excess weight! I used to think that I could eat anything and everything! If they sold the the food in a supermarket — it was made for human consumption. HOW BAD COULD IT BE?

Skinny Me: What Works!

My First Trip to a Gym to Build Muscle

A dear friend took me to a neighborhood gym and taught me how to lift free weights, bike on a computer-programmed bicycle, and run on a computer-programmed treadmill.

My friend had developed his own exercise routine based on the needs of his own body. How cool is that!

I realized that I had to learn how to design an exercise routine for myself!

My exercise mantra is:

Burn Fat! Build Muscle!

Lesson 1.
I learned how to design a cardio and weight-lifting routine:
- 5-10 Min. Cardio Warm-Up
- 25 Min. Weights
- 15 Min. Cardio: Run/Bike

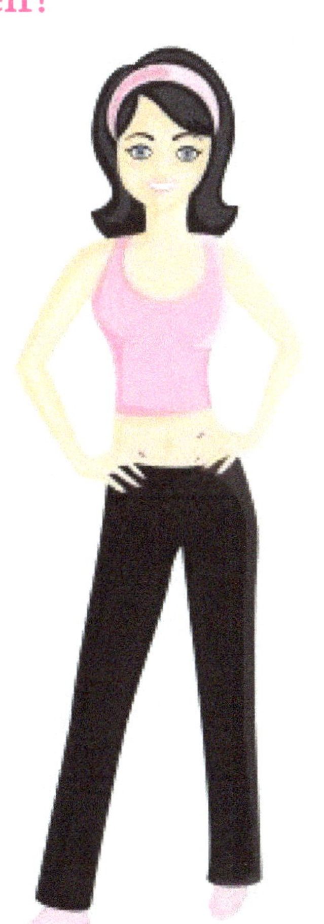

Lesson 2.
I learned that each weight-lifting routine consisted of 3 sets, and each set was 12-15 repetitions.

Lesson 3.
A gym buddy is great company! I listen to music to stay on track!

Lesson 4.
I learned how to make a tasty protein shake to refuel after a workout. Yum! Yum!

FAT ME: What Doesn't Work!

TV Couch Potato and Mindless Eating

Mindless eating while sitting on a couch watching a TV show or movie is how most people end up with a ring of fat around their waistline — or sitting in front of a computer screen.

What if I place an exercise bicycle in the TV room, and decide that I will spend time watching TV while biking and burning calories!

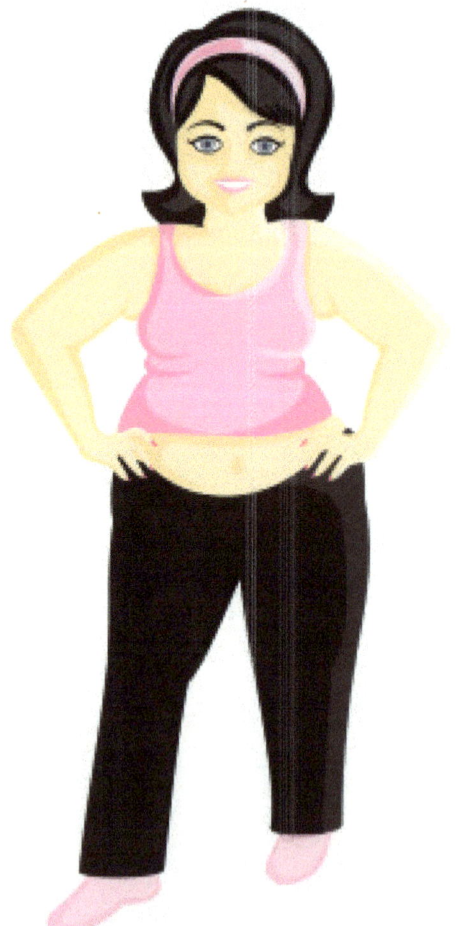

When you sign up at a gym, there is a TV set attached to every bike.

What if I set this up in my own home?

At least half the time watching a TV program is spent watching TV commercials. I always get up and do a chore during a commercial. 3-minute commercials are a great chuck of time to check laundry or vaccum a carpet — or lower the sound and meditate for 3 minutes.

Skinny Me: What Works!

Weight Lifting 101: My Muscle Groups

There are 600 muscles in my human body. There are 11 major muscle group in my body that need to be stretched out when I workout in the gym:

- **4 Arm Muscles** = 4 Excercises

  Forearm, Bicep, Tricep, and Shoulder

- **4 Core Muscles** = 4 Exercises

  Abs, Chest, Trapezius, and Latissimus Dorsi

- **3 Leg Muscles** = 3 Exercises

  Quadricept, Hamstring, and Calf

3 Strength Building Strategies:

- **Partial Repetitions**: You can't do any more repetitions with a full range of motion.

- **Drop Sets**: You reduce weight and continue to do repetitions.

- **Supersets**: You train two opposing muscle groups without resting.

- **Active Rests**: Don't sit around between sets, but hop on bike, do a plank or walk around gym.

Don't do too much too soon!
An injury can set you back for months. **Listen to you body**!

FAT ME: What Doesn't Work!

My 23 Excuses Not to Exercise

1. I'm not fit enough to exercise!
2. I don't like exercise!
3. It hurts to exercise!
4. It's boring!
5. I'm too tired!
6. Feeling sick!
7. Just ate!

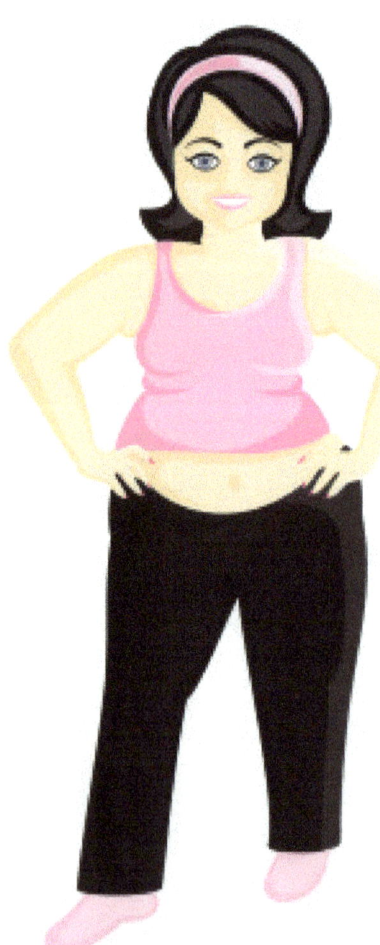

8. Too late!
9. No time!
10. Weather – Rain!
11. Weather – Too cold!
12. Weather – Snow!
13. Feel sore!
14. Left work too late!
15. Planning to work out tomorrow!
16. Worked out yesterday!
17. Got other plans!
18. Hangover!
19. Rest week!
20. Too hungry!
21. Don't want to work out in public!
22. Planning early night!
23. Dark outside!

Skinny Me: What Works!

My 25 Reasons to Exercise

1. Improves my quality of life!
2. Improves oxygen supply to cells!
3. Improves concentration!
4. Increases energy & endurance!
5. Reduces feelings of depression!
6. Decreases osteoporosis risk!
7. Prevents muscle loss!
8. Increases sports performance!
9. Lifts my mood!
10. Builds self-esteem!
11. Keeps my brain fit!
12. Boosts mental health!
13. Keeps body fit & able!
14. Boosts immune system!
15. Reduces stress!
16. Has anti-aging effects!
17. Improves skin tone & color!
18. Boosts productivity!
19. Boosts creative thinking!
20. Improves body image!
21. Gives you confidence!
22. Helps keep you focused!
23. Increases longevity!
24. Strengthens your bones!
25. Strengthens your heart!

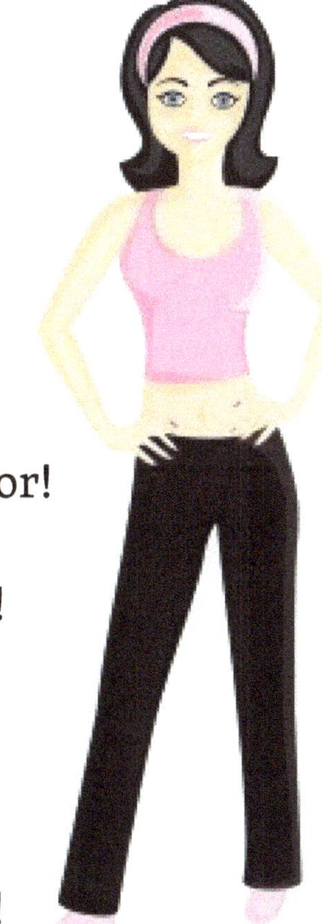

FAT ME: What Doesn't Work!

My Daily Food Journal of Whole Foods

I started to keep track of every morsel of food that I placed into my mouth. Losing weight is not about starving my body of essential nutrients. Losing weight is about feeding my body the essential nutrients to help it convert whole foods into energy for life & living!

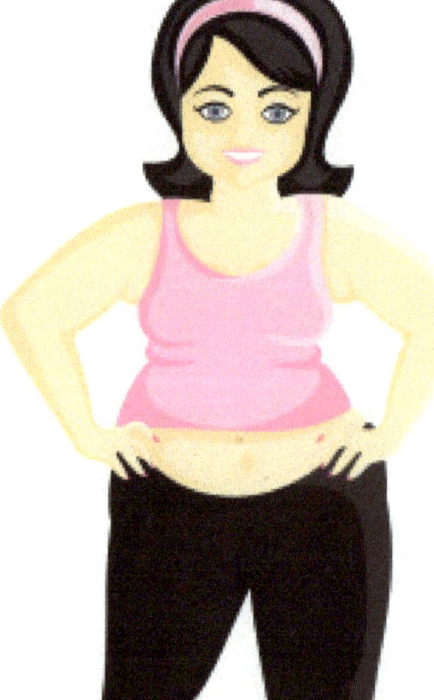

- Monday: 3/4 Veggies & 1/4 Chicken
- Tuesday: 3/4 Veggies & 1/4 Fish
- Wednesday: Veggie Platter
- Thursday: 3/4 Veggies & 1/4 Pasta
- Friday: 3/4 Veggies & 1/4 Grass-Fed Meat
- Saturday: Veggie Platter
- Sunday: Surprise

Lesson 1. Start the day on a full tank of energy — like filling up your car with gas.

Lesson 2. **Eat Small Meals**
Eat 5-7 small meals NOT one 5-course meal.

Lesson 3. **Hydrate All Day**
Drink at least 2 bottles of water!
ADD ELECTROLYTES!
(minerals: sodium, potassium, calcium, chlori magnesium, and phosphate.

Lesson 4. **I Love Leftovers**
Don't eat everything on your plate. Cut it in half or thirds, and take it hom

Skinny Me: What Works!

My Daily Exercise Journal
Aerobics, Arms, Abs, and Ass

I keep track of my regular exercise routine.
As I work out, my body is changing.
On day one, I am lifting 3-pound dumbbells.
After 30 days, I am lifting 5-pound dumbbells.
After 6 months, I am lifting 10-15 pound dumbbells.
Every day, I am stronger! Muscles are **SEXY!**

E-Z: One Exercise Bike and Two Dumbbells!

- Monday: Cardio & Weights
- Tuesday: Cardio & Weights
- Wednesday: Rest Day
- Thursday: Cardio & Weights
- Friday: Cardio & Weights
- Saturday: Rest Day
- Sunday: Cardio & Weights

Lesson 1. 2-Step Process
EXERTION & RECOVERY!
- Slow and Steady Moderate Exercise
- Don't Do Too Much Too Soon!
- Caution: Overuse Injuries
- Caution: Overtraining & Fatigue
- Use Epson Salt Baths for Recovery

Lesson 2. Listen to Music with Headphones

Lesson 3. Buildup Muscles!
After lifting weights, give muscles time
to rebuild to become bigger & stronger.
Anabolic: Buildup Muscles
Catabolic: Break Down Muscles

Lesson 4. Tone or Bulk?
Tone: Low Weight and High Repetitions
Bulk: High Weight and Low Repetitions

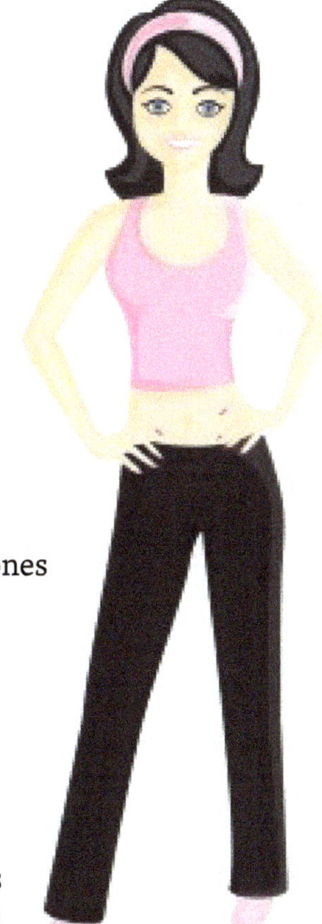

Lesson 5. Hydrate: 1 liter during exercise and 1 liter after exercise.

FAT ME: What Doesn't Work!

The Past is in the Past! 30, 60, 90 Days

My eating habits began in childhood and I am not to blame for the choices that my parents made. They made sure that I cleaned my plate and never wasted a morsel of food — especially because there are children starving in Africa!

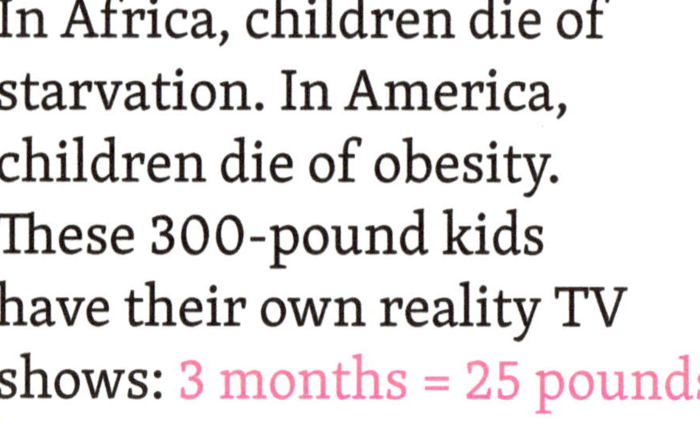

In Africa, children die of starvation. In America, children die of obesity. These 300-pound kids have their own reality TV shows: 3 months = 25 pounds!

2 Pounds a Week is Good!

They stop guzzling down sugary soda, and start drinking celery water!

My New Normal: 30, 60, 90 Days

- It takes 30 DAYS — to set a new habit into motion

- It takes 60 DAYS — to fine tune a new habit

- It takes 90 DAYS — to put a new habit on autopiolet

Skinny Me: What Works!

My New Normal: 30, 60, 90 Days

1. SELF-LOVE Is Not Selfish: SELF-LOVE Is TRUE LOVE!
2. Create a new relationship to food: ENERGIZE!
3. Check my morning POOP! Hotdog POOP = I am hydrated!
4. Hydrate! Thirst Is First! (lemon, ginger, hint of honey).
5. **Eat Whole Foods**! Nutrient-dense foods loaded with vitamins & minerals. Always wash pesticides off fruits & vegetables. Eat grass-fed beef! Eat wild-caught fish!
6. Eliminate foods with misleading ingredient labels!
7. Eat fiber-rich meals to stabilize blood sugar and eliminate food cravings & food addictions!
8. Timed Eating: Use food or store as fat!
9. Never leave home on an empty stomach!
10. Moderation or Elimination? Hard Choices!
11. Eat on a small plate.
12. Cut in thirds — eat smaller portions.
13. Take smaller bites: nibble & nosh.
14. Take a multi-vitamin.
15. Burn Fat! Build Muscle!
    Exertion & Recovery! Epson-salt baths!
16. Eating-Out Etiquette: Eat half & take the leftovers home or share an entree
    Order: baked, roasted, steamed, or poached
    Avoid: fried, deep-fried, breaded, and crispy
17. No caffeine after 5 p.m.
18. Snack on fresh vegetables:
    apples slices, celery sticks & humus
    baby carrots, red peppers & humus
19. RELAX: Listen to beautiful music!
20. STRESS: Avoid negative people!
21. Take a SELFIE! You earned it!
22. Go to sleep early. Repeat!

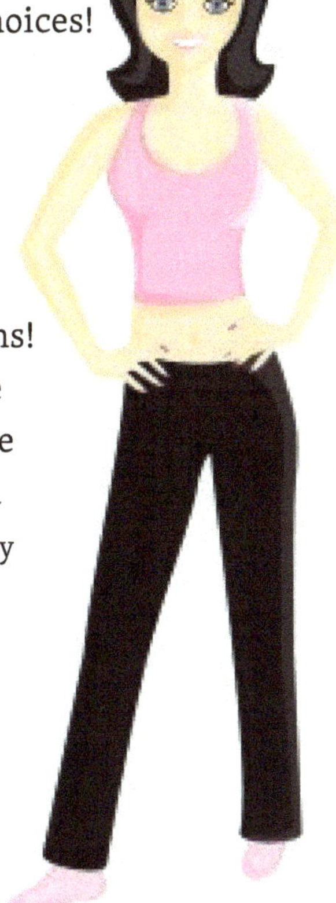

SHARON ESTHER LAMPERT
SEE THE WORLD THROUGH THE EYES OF A CREATIVE GENIUS

NYU
Honored Sharon Esther Lampert
with an Award for "Multi-Interdisciplinary Studies"
(YOUTUBE video)

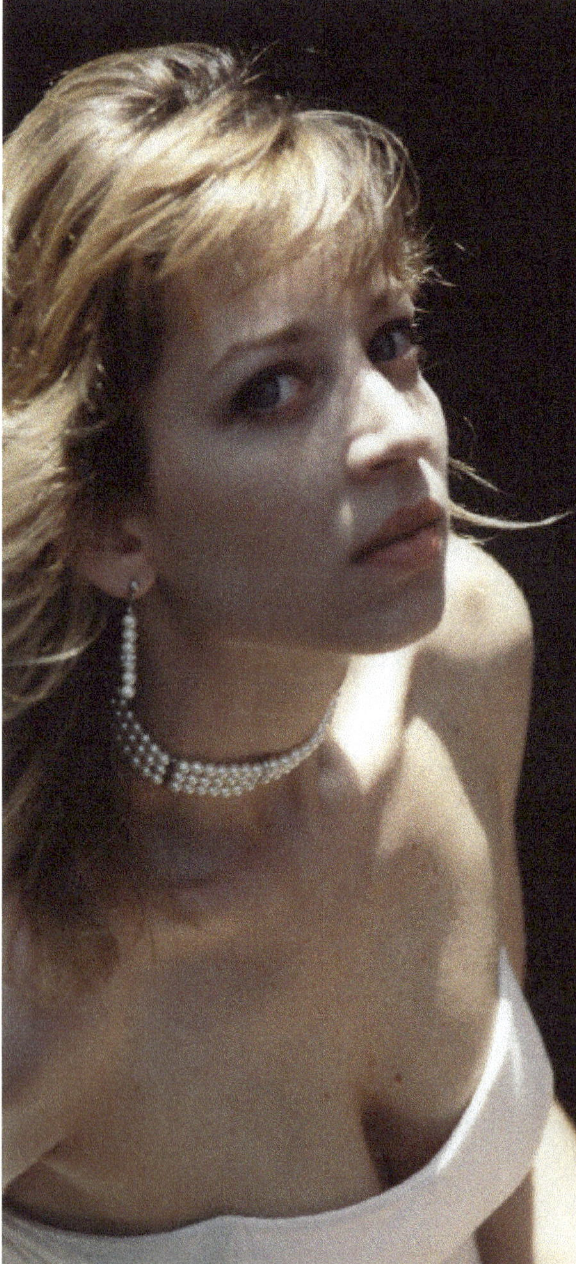

Poet
Philosopher
Peacemaker
Prophet
Princess and Pea
Pinup
Performer: Vocalist
Player: Jock
Paladin of Education
PHOTON SUPERHERO
Princess Kadimah
President
Publisher
Producer
Psychobiologist
Piano-Playing Cat
Phoenix
Prodigy

Websites:
- SharonEstherLampert.com
- WorldFamousPoems.com
- PoetryJewels.com
- PhilosopherQueen.com
- GodIsGoDo.com
- Schmaltzy.com
- TrueLoveBurnsEternal.com
- SillyLittleBoys.com
- WinAtThin.com
- BooksArePowerful.com
- HappyGrandparenting.com
- WritersRunTheWorld.com

Education:
SMARTGRADES BRAIN POWER REVOLUTION
- Smartgrades.com
- EverydayanEasyA.com
- PhotonSuperhero.com
- BooksNotBombs.com

Publish Books;
- PalmBeachBookPublisher.com
- MiamiBookPublisher.com

Sharon Esther Lampert

Gifted: Born with an Extra Body Part, a "Creative Apparatus"

PRODIGY

Unleash The Creator The God Within: 10 Esoteric Laws of Genius & Creativity

PROPHET

The 22 Commandments: All You Will Ever Know About God

Who Knew God Was a Chatterbox: A Working Definition of God — GOD IS GO! DO!

POET

One of the World's Greatest Poets — 18 Books of Poetry

POETRY WORLD RECORD: 120 WORDS OF RHYME

The Greatest Poems Ever Written on Extraordinary World Events

http://famouspoetsandpoems.com/poets.html

PHILOSOPHER QUEEN

- God of What? 11 Esoteric Laws of Inextricability — Is Life a Gift or a Punishment?
- Temporary Insanity: We Are Building Our Lives on a Sand Trap —Written in Letter S
- Women Have All the Power But Have Never Learned How to Use It
- Sperm Manifesto: 10 Rules for the Road

PEACEMAKER

WORLD PEACE EQUATION.COM

PALADIN OF EDUCATION — **25 Books**

SMARTGRADES BRAIN POWER REVOLUTION

- THE SILENT CRISIS DESTROYING AMERICAS BRIGHTEST MINDS
- EVERY DAY AN EASY A!

PHOTON SUPERHERO

SUPERHERO OF EDUCATION

www.PhotonSuperhero.com

PIONEER

- SILLY LITTLE BOYS: 40 RULES OF MANHOOD
- LOVE YOU MORE THAN YESTERDAY — 14 Relationship Strategies
- CUPID Language of Love — Written in Letter C
- PUBLISH: THE SECRET SAUCE OF BOOK SALES — Written in Letter P
- DESTINY: Are You Living Life by Default or by Design? — Written in Letter D
- THERAPY: Every Day You Have to Take a Test! — Written in Letter T
- WIN AT THIN — Written in Letter A

PERFORMER

Vocalist (YOUTUBE Videos)

PRINCESS KADIMAH

8TH PROPHETESS OF ISRAEL: THE 22 COMMANDMENTS

PINUP

SEXIEST CREATIVE GENIUS IN HUMAN HISTORY

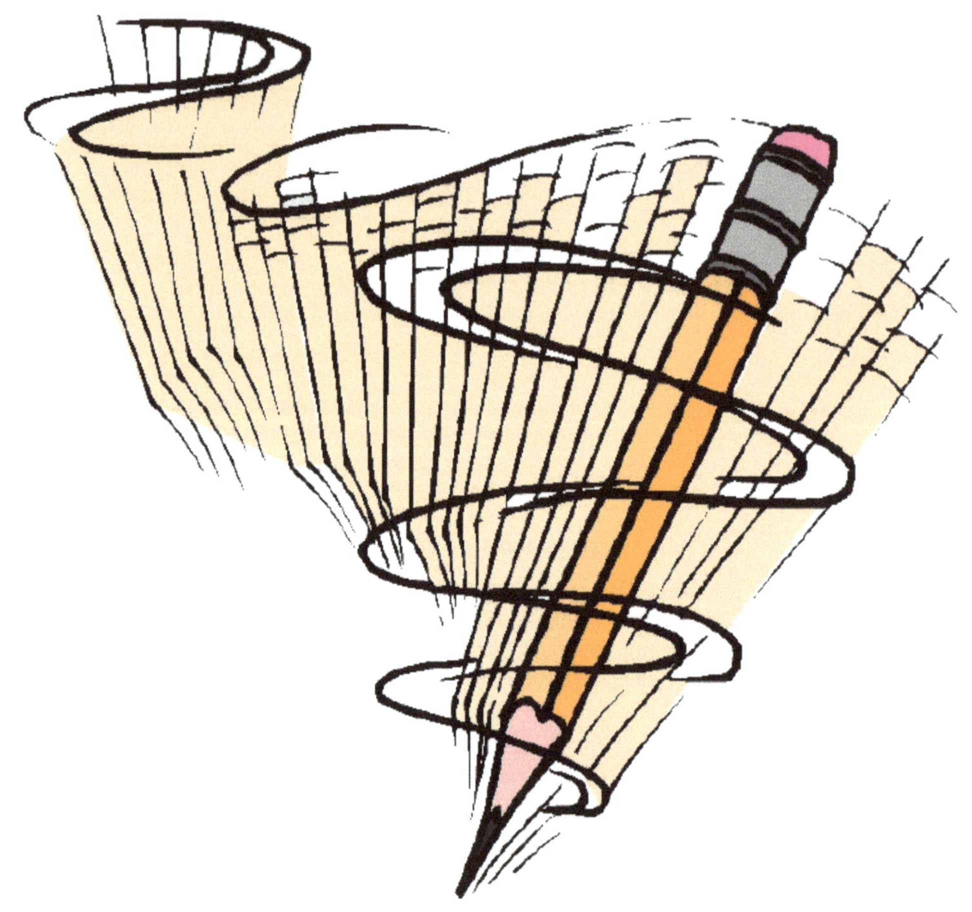

I Am Mortal.
My Books Are Immortal.
Please Handle My Books Gently.
My Books Are My Remains.

This book was compiled in four parts:
Part 1. Birth of Idea — 2015
Part 2. Format Book — 2019
Part 3. Essays: May 2022
Part 4. Publish Book — May 2023

Sharon Esther Lampert

SEE THE WORLD THROUGH THE EYES OF A CREATIVE GENIUS

Poet, Prophet, Philosopher, Peacemaker, Princess & Pea, Prodigy

www.ingramcontent.com/pod-product-compliance
Lightning Source LLC
Chambersburg PA
CBHW050018040726
47599CB00014B/1451